HARRY SMITH & STEVE CRUCHON

INSTANT
Bowling

GROSSET & DUNLAP · *Publishers* · NEW YORK

ISBN: 0-448-01515-3

1977 PRINTING

THANKS AND APPRECIATION

The authors are grateful for the assistance given by so many to *Instant Bowling*. Special thanks go to the Brunswick Corporation, particularly Harry Grove, public relations manager, and Lou Vrana of Grove's staff; and to the members of Brunswick's Advisory Staff Of Champions, notably Pete Carter and Bill Srock, both of whom have well-deserved reputations as outstanding bowling instructors.

About the Authors

STEVE CRUCHON

Steve Cruchon is a rare combination of star bowler and award-winning writer. For more than a quarter of a century, he has been a member of leading teams in the Detroit All-Star Classic, held by many to be the most powerful bowling league in the country, and served as team captain on several occasions. His many bowling championships include an all-time record smash of 1180 for five games — an average of 236 per game — in the venerable *Detroit Times* Singles Classic.

Under Cruchon's editorship *The Detroit Modern Bowler* has won countless national "best" awards. Cruchon himself has received awards and commendations beyond count. Easily one of the nation's foremost tenpin chroniclers, Cruchon's oft-quoted work appears regularly in national publications.

A consistent winner in the annual American Bowling Congress' writers' contest, Cruchon's awards in recent years also have included the *Mort Luby Distinguished Service Award* (per-haps the top award in the country for bowling writers), and "Bowling's Man Of The Year" awards from the Bowling Proprietors Association of Greater Detroit and the Greater Detroit Bowling Association.

Cruchon is a member of the Detroit Bowling Hall Of Fame and a past president of the Bowling Writers Association of America. *Sports Illustrated* has singled him out, among a handful of authorities, as one "... whose criticisms and ideas have had a marked influence on the game."

HARRY SMITH

Harry Smith's remarkable achievements on the lanes have won for him a singular position among the very elite of the bowling world. Born in 1930, in Cleveland, Ohio, Smith began to bowl when he was 12 years old. He was still in his teens when he gained national recognition.

In 1955, after two years in the Army, he left the Cleveland area and moved to Detroit

to join the Pfeiffer team. A year later he became a member of the Stroh team in Detroit. The following season he joined the Falstaff team of St. Louis, remaining with that club until 1963. The Pfeiffer, Stroh, and Falstaff teams are considered among the greatest bowling teams of all time. Smith conducts bowling schools when he's not out winning championships. He is an experienced teacher of the sport, having conducted instruction clinics for Brunswick Corporation, as a member of Brunswick's Advisory Staff Of Champions, throughout all of the 50 states.

Smith's accomplishments as a bowler include American Bowling Congress tournament titles, Professional Bowlers Association "Open," the ABC Masters' crown, the All-Star championship, and many national match titles. It follows that he is a perennial All-American.

Smith is also seen on television. In 1959, he won $22,500 in a half hour's appearance on a nationally televised bowling show. He has bowled more than 50 perfect games. He has rolled series of 879 (300-300-279) and 889 (300-299-290).

A charter member of the Professional Bowlers Association, Smith's money-winning record since the start of the PBA tourney tours in 1958 tops that of any other professional ace.

Contents

The things that bowling does for one!

King Of The Family Games

There was a time, only a couple of decades ago, when the standard admonishments of a mother to one or more of her brood included, " . . . and don't let me catch you going into a bowling alley."

This always tickled Dad, who knew no one would let any of the kids into a tenpin parlor anyway. The doors opened reluctantly and beer-frosted mustaches quivered indignantly even when Mom bravely took one of her rare flings at the pins.

Less than half a century ago bowling was a game meant almost exclusively for men. Equipment, environment and atmosphere all strongly suggested Men Only, and few of the uninvited were tempted enough to trespass.

The components of the game, the many parts which lend to its vast appeal, are such that no one gender—men, for example— could possibly have kept it bottled up for their own use for very long. Sooner or later the cork had to pop and the contents perforce spill out and spread as they have into the far corners of untold homes throughout the breadth of the land.

Which came first in bowling—women and children, or the great transition that saw the game grow from a tough, crude, often unkempt upstart to a respected gentleman of stature decked out in distinctive, high-toned garb? Did women and children prompt the change in bowling? Or did the change lead women and children to the game? Like the one about the chicken and the egg, the answer is moot, of course, but the point is that bowling has become a full-blown game for the entire family, and each day sees it becoming more and more entrenched as such.

In bowling *togetherness* is all over the place, laying there right out in the open in big piles waiting to be scooped up. Mom, who long has known a trick or two with broom and mop, now has picked up some bowling know-how. She has become at least passably adept, enough to feel pride and a sense of accomplishment at cleaning up on the pins. On the

Bowling is Togetherness . . . the ideal pastime for families.

lanes, Mom and Dad and the kids enjoy friendly rivalry and share fun. At home, there is a lot more to talk about and laugh over, to plan and anticipate. Beyond bowling together in "open" play day or night around the calendar, there are countless leagues and tournaments of all descriptions in which any two or more members of a family can band and vie for trophies and other prizes.

Boredom? Loneliness? Neither is known in bowling. Educators, doctors and the clergy have nothing but high praise for the game. They speak glowingly of the many benefits in it for individuals and families as a whole. Bowling contributes to physical and mental health, affects character, combats delinquency.

From 8 to 80, it's "what the doctor ordered," say the doctors themselves.

The modern bowling site figures importantly in everyday community life. It has become a civic recreation center, a wholesome place for families to spend happy hours together, a favorite rendezvous to make a date and meet and make new friends. For oldsters the tenpin center is a haven where one forgets the years, and hours are given wings.

Sometimes bowling comes out looking like cupid. It not only keeps families together . . . it helps make *new* ones. A mixed league in Detroit produced no less than seven marriages among members who had started the season as strangers!

My How You've Grown

Bowling dates back to medieval times, but the "modern" version of tenpins—the game we know today—got its start within many of our own lifetimes. The first American style bowling alley was built in New York in the early 1880s by "Uncle" Joe Thum, a jovial tavern owner. Thum added two (his two crudely built basement lanes) and two (companionship and recreation) together and got what has evolved into a tremendously popular sport with millions of devotees the world over.

In the fledgling days bowling (the modernized tenpin variety) was a boon companion to saloons, a sideline activity that took place in cold, damp basements or in dreary adjoining rooms. Today the game is big business and a major sport accorded the same towering recognition granted to baseball, football and golf.

Compared with the kegling hovels of yesteryear, present-day tenpin plants are like ivory-towered Taj Mahals that at once lure and delight. One can see these elegant, million-dollar layouts almost everywhere. They stretch out to as many as a hundred or more lanes in an uninterrupted line, plush sites of refinement and fetching decor, offering every comfort and convenience.

Bowling is growing so fast around the globe that it is impossible to keep an accurate, up-to-date count of the number of people who play at it and benefit from it. The United States alone, the unchallenged hotbed of tenpins, boasts of at least 30 million bowlers (add another couple of hundred thousand or so in a few months). There are about nine million woman bowlers and over a million kid bowlers, but this or any census of the giant, sprawling tenpin clan is quickly rendered obsolete by the constant, compounding growth of the game and the number of adherants. Locales may differ but the essence of bowling, the basic conditions and rules, the game's appeal, the reactions of bowlers, are all of a universal sameness.

Today's bowling centers rival the palaces of storyland.

Various associations guide and govern the game, give it unity, uniformity, strength and character. These staunch pillars, without which bowling would grope and stumble with little or no real direction, are the American Bowling Congress (ABC), founded in 1895; Woman's International Bowling Congress (WIBC), started in 1961, and the Bowling Proprietors Association of America (BPAA), organized in 1932.

Also important in bowling's present scheme of things are the American Junior Bowling Congress, which had its beginning in 1935 and is now under the joint guardianship of the ABC and WIBC, and a pair of mere infants—the ABC-handled United States Seniors' Bowling Association, inaugurated in 1959, and the BPAA Youth Bowling Association, formed in 1963. The BPAA has its own Seniors' program which was introduced in 1963.

As their names indicate, these non-profit organizations take in both sexes and all age extremes.

Another force for good in bowling is the Professional Bowlers' Association (PBA), a product of bowling's new "jet age," started in 1958. The PBA, which lists virtually all of the game's headliners as members, at once provides distinction and an incentive for its minority flock. Until the PBA came along the boundary separating pros and amateurs in bowling was an obscure, controversial one with broad interpretations. The PBA has carved deep, clear lines to point out its side of the professional-amateur border. No longer is there promiscuous sauntering into someone else's bowling pasture. Nowadays a pro is a pro and an amateur is an amateur, and the twain meet only in the dreams of an amateur.

Women have their own professional status. Organized in the Professional Women's Bowling Association, the fair sex has developed into far more than that in bowling. These days the scores of many women often match and sometimes even surpass the lofty scores of male stars.

Bowling's unity is perhaps best illustrated in the National Bowling Council, organized in 1943. The NBC is supported by the various segments of the bowling industry. It acts as a clearing house and sounding board for all integers of the game, resolving mutual problems and working toward overall betterment.

Electronics and automation have also played key roles in the zoom of tenpins. With air-conditioning we now enjoy automatic pinsetters, electric foul detectors, electronic air filters, screen-like scoreboards, electric hand-dryers, an electronically controlled device which identifies pins and, on the same illuminated panel, shows the bowler the course his ball should follow on spare shots, and a dozen like innovations heralding the bright new world of tenpins.

Bowling owes thanks, too, to the equipment manufacturers—notably the two goliaths of the industry—Brunswick Corporation (over 100 years old) and American Machine & Foundry Co. (AMF). These two firms alone have spent millions in bowling research and promotion.

The advent of the automatic pinspotter—invented in 1936, introduced to the public in 1946, and in volume production by 1951—brought an orderly regulation to the game, hurried the exit of the pinboy (a throw-back to the days when bowling was in kneebritches) and, at the same time, activated a major boom. This in turn attracted some of the best business brains in the country, sparked new ideas and technique, brought dignity and "class." With each passing year new peaks are reached and the game's horizon keeps broadening.

Striking It Rich

These are times of unprecedented harvest, the likes of which the grand old game of toppling tenpins has never seen.

Less than two decades ago when a headline bowler earned as much as $1,000 in any one year he considered himself fortunate. Now a top level player can earn more than that every month without pushing his luck and talent too far. It's enough to make mothers forget the presidency and raise their sons to be professional bowlers.

Many of today's top stars receive anywhere from $50,000 to more than $100,000 per annum for their ability to guide a bowling ball with telling effect. On the other hand, millions of bowlers gladly pay to roll the same round object down the same smooth and shining pathway at the same lively, bottle-shaped pieces of maple . . . getting nothing in return but the compelling urge to do it again and again.

Like baseball, you can't beat bowling's hours and pay. Thousands of dollars can be won in an hour or two of tournament competition, or in mere minutes on television. The latter, exposing bowling to millions who perhaps have never seen it close up, helped give the game a big push toward its present high-stationed popularity and affluency. Bowling's stars have become noted, easily-recognized, autograph-signing personages who won't trade their places in the sun with Hollywood's personalities.

Even comparative beginners averaging less than 150, aided and abetted by handicaps (pins added to their scores), have been known to help themselves to great riches from bowling's treasure house. Women do all right at it, too. Marion Ladewig, Grand Rapids, Mich., grandmother who is one of the game's immortals, squeezes more than $25,000 a year out of her bowling ball.

Therman Gibson displays the form that enabled him to win $75,000 on a single, half-hour, nationally televised bowling show.

No longer is security a will-o-the-wisp for bowlers. The earnings of bowlers now rate with the reassuring yearly stipends received by major league baseball players, professional golfers and professional football stars.

Almost anyone can become a good bowler and, considering the element of chance and luck so prevalent in bowling, nearly anyone who knows anything at all about the basic fundamentals of the game has the same golden opportunity to make a small fortune firing ball against pins. Yet those who never win a dime at it, and by this token will never have their amateur standing seriously questioned, reap perhaps the most valuable of bowling rewards.

Getting The Most Out Of Bowling

The secret of bowling's deep-down appeal is that it can be enjoyed by all, no matter one's sex, age, shape, condition, station or ability.

Proficiency has its own compensations and is a common goal, of course, and the primary purpose of this book is to help one acquire tenpin know-how quickly and easily. But in bowling proficiency and enjoyment are not necessarily related.

Regardless of average, high or low, you are bound to have pleasant company with whom you will share an emotional affinity. Your bowling pals will laugh when you laugh, moan when you moan, exult when you exult. They'll pat you on the back, encourage, holler "Atta boy!", show sympathy, or heckle in a way that further demonstrates friendship.

In bowling everybody gets in the act. The stage is open to all, and each role is of relative equal importance.

What other sport offers as much?

Even if you are an out-and-out newcomer you will find it a simple matter to start bowling and, if you wish, join a league where you will feel at ease and be able to bask in the good fellowship which always has been an integral part of the game.

If you have never bowled, and want to, merely walk into any bowling center and tell the person at the service counter that you want a lane. Let the person know it is your first attempt. Ask him, or her, to help you find a proper-fitting ball among the dozens of "house" balls resting on the ball returns and ball racks. Rent a pair of bowling shoes. Ask how to keep score. So you get off on the right foot, ask to be shown at least the rudiments of the game.

While your bowling career can be launched in the manner just described, it is best to make your initial attempt in the company of one or more friends who know something about the correct basic fundamentals of bowling. It will help make you feel more at ease and less self conscious, and you might absorb more.

After you have had a few games under your belt and start to get the feel of things, you will find that certain crude essentials will start falling in place by themselves. In no time at all you'll be talking tenpin language and going about the business of toppling tenpins like an old trouper—and loving every minute of it.

There are leagues of all kinds for bowlers of all kinds. Joining one is as easy as saying, "I want to bowl in a league." Just make your wish known—in a bowling center, in shop or office, at club, church or school.

Leagues are made up of millionaires and laborers, doctors and machinists, merchants and hod carriers, teachers and truck drivers, politicians and plumbers. There are leagues for tots as young as five, for oldsters up to a hundred, for the blind, and for those whose world is a wheelchair.

Leagues are as easy to organize as they are to join.

Here's all there is to it:

Round up a group of from 10 persons on up, break up the group into teams of about equal strength, get a set of rules to follow from either the American Bowling Congress or the Woman's International Bowling Congress, elect officers, set up a handicap plan of some sort if you want to make the competition even more equal, pick out a night (or an afternoon) and a site—and go to it. Any bowling estab-

Bowling is the only major sport in which it is not necessary to own your own equipment to participate. If you bowl regularly, it is advisable to own your bowling shoes as well as your own ball. Street shoes are out. Those who bowl only on occasion may, if they wish, rent sanitized, hygienic bowling shoes for a small fee at the service counter of any tenpin site.

Most bowling plants have ball-fitting devices where you can be measured for your own ball quickly, accurately and conveniently.

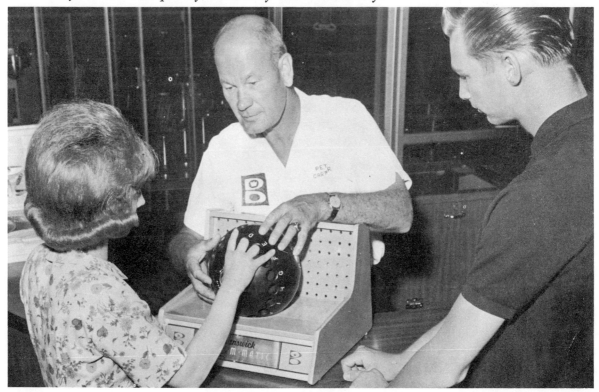

lishment will give you all the additional help you might need.

It has been proved until it has become a cliche that leagues make for better workers, more cooperative students, happier club members. They create friends, enhance sociability, place a premium on sportsmanship, courtesy, tolerance, consideration for others.

A word of caution should be inserted at this point. Before one travels too far down the tenpin road and perchance falls into harmful habits of bowling that might be hard to break later, the novice is strongly advised to seek out a competent instructor who at, or near, the outset will chart a proper course for him or her to follow.

Keep in mind that one can't learn to bowl entirely from a book. There are no short cuts to becoming a star. It takes dedication and application.

When you practice, and for your own bowling welfare it should be often, practice with a definite purpose. Do the right things, as directed by a bona-fide instructor, or in keeping with what is graphically pointed out in these pages. Contained herein is the distilled product of years of trial and error, bowling knowledge culled from long experience. If you are a greenhorn, pick out what suits you best and feels the most natural. And stick to it! Get to know your weaknesses, find the remedies here and practice until the flaws are corrected.

Styles and methods may vary but the prime requisites are of one mold. Bowlers should strive not to mimic but to put their own natural traits to good use, shying away from that which only serves to hinder and confuse rather than aid and enlighten. Bowling requires no more than simple, natural functions—i.e.,

Keeping score is as easy as elementary arithmetic, which is exactly what it is. If you are a newcomer, the bowling center manager, or an employee of the site, or anybody who has ever bowled before and is near by, will show you how it's done in one minute.

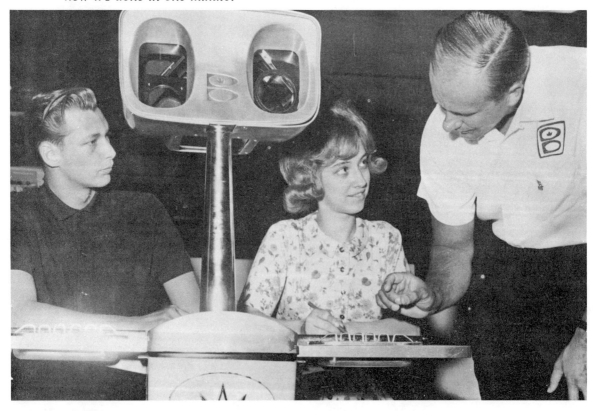

In bowling, the beginner is as welcome as an old hand. There's always a qualified person on the premises from whom you can pick up at least the basic fundamentals. Later, when you have become more acclimated to the game, seek out a bona-fide instructor who will set a proper course for you to follow.

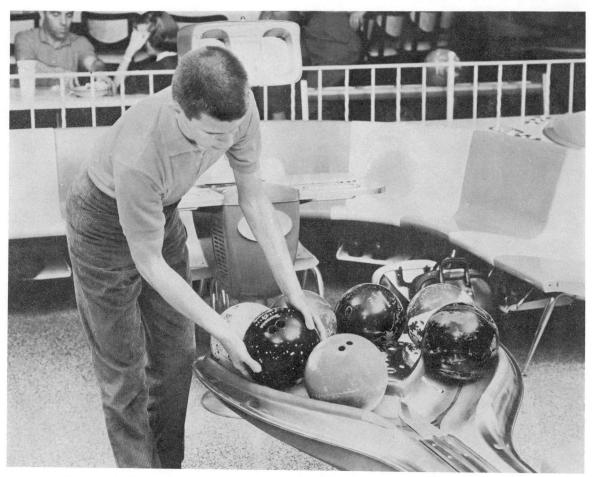

Every bowling center has a wide assortment of bowling balls available for use. For safety's sake, pick up balls from ball return in the manner shown here.

walking, swinging one's arm, taking aim, rolling a ball in a specific direction. Stripped, bowling is as easy and uncluttered as that. It is only when one takes on too much "excess baggage" that the game becomes a weighty project.

Don't worry too much what to wear when bowling. There's no need to be a fashion-plate. Just wear what is neat and presentable, what feels loose and comfortable and doesn't bind or restrict movement of arms, legs and body.

You don't *have* to own your own equipment but you'll get infinitely more out of bowling if you do. With your own bowling shoes and bowling ball comes added comfort, confidence and pleasure.

Proper footwork is vital and best achieved when you own your own bowling shoes. They affect rhythm, balance, coordination, smoothness, etc. They cushion your delivery, make for a sure-footed approach, enable you to properly slacken and "brake" your slide. Too, the heels of bowling shoes are of a type of rubber that doesn't mark up or deface the floors of approach areas.

The importance of having your own bowling ball cannot be overemphasized. No one, not even an established star, can reach consistent heights with a ball chosen at random, one that is not ideally suited to the shape of one's hand and conforms with one's own "feel" and grip.

A confident, comfortable grip is the foundation, the first principle, of good bowling.

Even the great often feel the need of, and request, power and know-how beyond their own to help them on the lanes. This prize-winning photo shows Shirley Garms winning the 1961 All-Star tournament before a gallery of thousands in Miami Beach.

How A Bowling Ball Should Fit And Be Held

Bowling balls are like people; no two of them are exactly alike.

As shapes of hands differ, and physical get-ups which effect bowling styles vary, so, too, is one bowling ball different from another.

Regulation bowling balls, conforming with ABC specifications, are all of the same mould, of course, but the manner in which holes are drilled into bowling balls is endlessly at odds.

ABC regulations say that a bowling ball must weigh not more than 16 pounds nor less than 10 pounds. Surprisingly, not all of the stars use a full 16-pounder. Some use 15-pound balls—pointing out that they can handle a lighter ball easier, which is important, and that their "stuff" (action of the ball when it hits the pins) is not lessened. But they comprise a definite minority. Most of the better bowlers use a full-weight ball. Still, they advise beginners to use a lightweight model—but never under 14 pounds for a man and 12 pounds for a woman, if they find it easier to handle and control. The main thought here is that you should rule the ball; the ball should never rule or "throw" you.

In days gone by, almost all bowlers used two-finger balls. They had no other choice. That's all there was to use. As the game progressed the trend swung to three-finger balls. Now the two-finger ball is a rarity. The explanation is simple: A three-finger ball is easier to hold, feels more comfortable, is dropped less often, controlled better, and there is less strain on the fingers. One can't ask for more than that from a bowling ball.

A ball that fits properly is one that has finger holes that aren't too tight or too loose.

The span doesn't stretch the hand or cause squeezing or pinching, placing undue stress on fingers. The pitch (the angle in which the holes are drilled in relation to the center of the ball) allows an unhampered, free and easy release of the fingers and thumb.

Proper pitch depends on style of delivery, manner of release and the type of "working" ball one rolls.

It is wisest to leave such complex things as pitch—in fact, the *entire* fitting of a ball—almost wholly in the hands of qualified experts.

An improperly fitted ball can bring on blisters, swollen and painful finger joints and knuckles and, obviously, can wreck control.

How can you tell if a ball fits right? Well, the standard procedure is to insert your thumb into the ball to about three-quarters of its length, then lay your hand flat on the surface of the ball, extending your middle finger over the middle finger hole. The center crease of the finger should be about a quarter of an inch past the inside edge of the hole. Do the same with the second finger. If the finger and thumbhole sizes are as they should be, you will find the fingers and thumb will fit in the holes comfortably, with just enough play to allow you to let go of the ball with maximum ease and effectiveness.

There is an endless variety of bowling grips. Besides the Conventional Grip, the better known grips are Finger Tip Grip, Semi-Finger Tip Grip, Chuck Collier Grip, Ned Day Grip, Sully Bates Grip, Curval Grip, Easter Grip and Shur-Hook Grip. Dozens more leap into mind, but these will hold you for the time being.

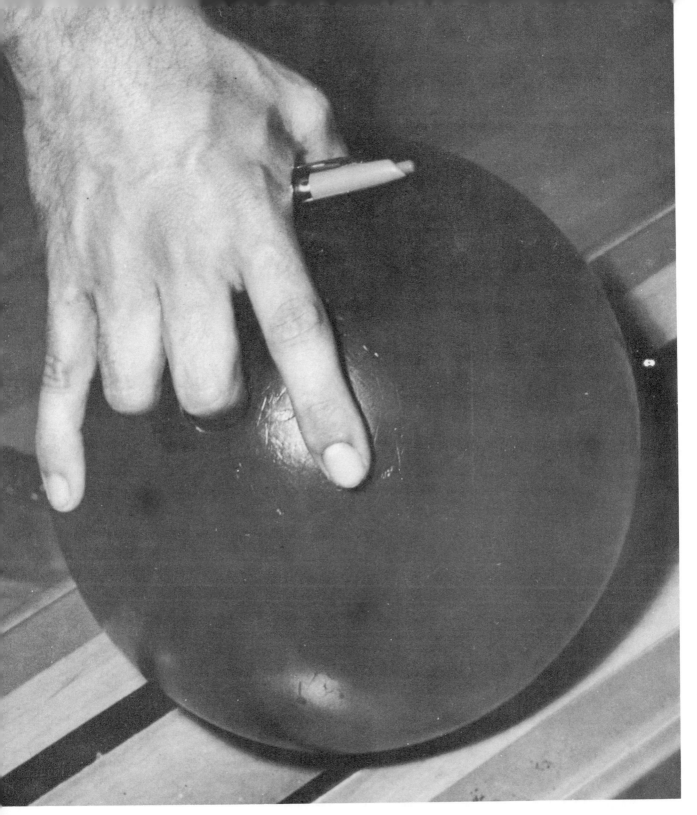

You've a good fit if you can insert a pencil, without forcing, under the palm of your hand when gripping the ball.

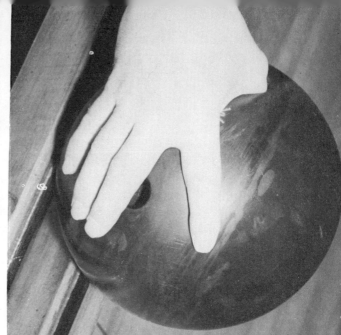

A ball that fits one's hand properly is one where, among other things, the thumb and finger holes are loose enough for an easy, unhampered release.

How can you tell if the span is right? Place your hand on top of the ball, thumb fully inserted. Second crease of the middle finger should be just over the inner edge of the finger hole.

When the span is too narrow (left), the ball is squeezed or pinched; when too wide (right), the hand is stretched. Avoid both. They place undue stress and strain on fingers, hinder and adversely affect smooth release and consistent control.

It is ridiculous but nonetheless true that one can grow grey in bowling just over grips. To eliminate confusion and some of the "excess baggage" we talked about earlier, we will explain only the more commonly used grips, and do it as briefly and as simply as possible.

In the Conventional Grip the thumb is drilled on the centerline of the ball. The finger holes are drilled at equal distances to the right and left of centerline.

The finger Tip and Semi-Finger Tip Grips have extra wide spans in which the ball is gripped at or near the first joint of the thumb and first joints of the fingers. The holes are lined up as in the Conventional Grip. Pitch varies according to length of span.

In the Curval Grip the finger holes are drilled so that they bend and arc inward toward the thumb, imparting a handle-like grip.

Other grips offer additional variations in the positioning of finger holes and in the pitch or slant of the finger holes.

A ball's balance often determines the man-

Note how securely the ball is held on the backswing. This shows the importance of proper fit and grip. Holding 16 pounds (the weight of the ball) straight out in back of you, even though gravity and momentum do enter the picture, is made easier if you have a good hold on it. Make sure your grip is right for you!

Young Judy Audsley, one of the nation's best distaff bowlers, points out proper grip fundamentals to a group of teen-agers. In the standard Conventional Grip the fingers are spread out naturally, thumb inserted about three-quarters length, with enough "play" in all of the finger holes for an easy, unrestricted release. Proper grip often is purely a matter of what "feels right".

ner in which it is, or should be, drilled. This in turn can affect one's grip. Balance also can influence the behaviour of the ball. Rank and file bowlers are warned about experimenting with and using anything but a conventionally balanced ball, if for no other reason than for the sake of rolling a ball that works the same on every toss. Balls balanced otherwise, including the "top weight" kind, are given to acting strangely with little provocation—like a slight change in hand action, for instance.

In keeping with the game's nonconformity, the top stars use a wide variety of grips.

The Finger Tip Grip and its first cousin, the Semi-Finger Tip Grip, while popular with many leading bowlers, are recommended only for skilled bowlers. Through years of experimenting with grips and pitches of all descriptions, experienced bowlers acquire the finesse needed to properly govern these, at times, unruly relatives of the granddaddy Conventional Grip.

Telling a bowler what grip he should use is like telling soccer fans to stay put. It's a waste of words.

Doing "what comes naturally" is a sound rule to heed at all times. Do not try to spread the fingers out too far, or keep them too close together. Don't "choke" the ball, or hold it in a sloppy manner. Just hold it naturally. Chances are it will be the correct way. And don't "bury" the thumb. Insert it so that the inner edge of the thumb is about mid-way between the first and second joints of the thumb. This will keep you from "locking" your thumb in the ball and will bring about an easier release.

Rookie bowlers are advised to use a Conventional Grip, or one not far removed from it, at least until they have become fairly well set in their bowling ways and are experienced enough to properly evaluate the various grips. Then they can judge which is the most suitable for their particular use.

Buzz Fazio's smooth swing and delivery stems from a sound starting stance. His feet are pointed straight ahead. The weight of his body is evenly distributed. He is firm, but not rigid . . . relaxed, but not limp.

The Starting Stance

Top bowlers agree that "timing" can make or break a bowler. The path to the foul-line, while short, is strewn with pitfalls if your timing is off.

Stance, footwork and release should be coordinated and made to mesh smoothly and effectively from start to finish of delivery.

Proper timing is not as complex or as difficult to achieve as it might sound. It merely means doing the right thing at the right time. When you do what you *should,* proper timing becomes automatic.

In the starting stance, approximately 12 feet from the foul-line (depending on the number and length of steps you take), it is recommended, but not held to be absolutely essential, that the body be moderately erect, leaning partially forward, with knees slightly bent. Shoulders should face the pins squarely, with weight distributed evenly on both feet.

Position of the feet is a matter of preference. They can be together, slightly apart, or one in front of the other. The ball, held anywhere between the belt and the chest, but always directly in front of you, should be supported almost entirely by the non-bowling hand. The distance to the foul-line should be long enough to give the bowler enough room to generate the momentum needed for a smooth, easy, unforced delivery.

While it has been recommended to stand near-erect when addressing the pins, the bowler may use whichever method he finds to be the most natural for him and which gives him the best results. There are stars who stoop or crouch when starting their deliveries.

Your starting position should be lined up with the head pin. Stand either squarely in line with it, or immediately to the right or left of it. Only at rare times, when there are extremes in lane conditions, should one ever go beyond those boundaries. It is a good idea always to take off from the same spot on the approach. This helps one achieve desired consistency. As you gain experience and learn how to "play" lanes, moving to right or left depending on how the lane and your ball "work," you will also learn to adjust your starting position a notch or two in one direction or the other on the approaches. Under *normal* lane conditions, most stars do what we have just said and now repeat: Stand either directly in line with, or just to the left or right of the head pin when assuming your stance.

Avoid stiffening up. Be calm, relaxed. Don't hurry your delivery. Be deliberate, precise. Get set, concentrate on the target—the 1–3 pocket or a spot on the lane in line with the pocket—and let'er roll.

Be careful not to turn your body sideways when preparing to start your stride. It likely will make you go up to the foul-line in anything but the proper straight path. When starting your delivery don't hold the ball up to where it obstructs vision, or down so low that your backswing will be stunted and forced.

At the beginning it might be wise to practice stance and stride without ball or pins. Just keep going through the correct motions. Do it until the start and the step order and their relation to the arm-swing and release have been mastered and are almost mechanical. (Succeeding chapters will discuss the proper fundamentals.)

Keep those shoulders straight!

Fine balance begins with one's starting stance. Bill Lillard keeps his elbows in close to his body for the support which helps tighten and lock in the perfect balance for which he is noted.

Use the stance that feels "old shoe" to you and produces the best results. Here's Pete Carter's unpretentious, business-like starting stance. Note how Carter holds the ball, poising it for grooved action.

First Move: The Pushaway

Dick Hoover's pushaway, shown well along its downward path, has much to do with his flawless forward motion and perfectly timed swing. He gently and slowly pushes the ball straight away from his body. The motion is never quick and jerky.

The pushaway, the "trigger" of the approach, can be likened to the "waggle" in golf. When executed properly the pushaway gives you a smooth, effortless start—setting other phases of your footwork in proper motion. A faulty pushaway can disrupt your timing, make your approach and release discordant instead of the symphony of smooth motion it should be.

If you carry the ball too long, neglecting to push it out and away from your body as you start your first step, you will find yourself ahead of the ball at the foul-line. This will make you swing the ball in a sidewise arc around your hip, which is contrary to the straight-back-straight-out swing advocated by champion bowlers.

If you drop the ball down too soon, it will cause your shoulder to sag, which in turn will force you to "sidearm" the ball and possibly drop it at the foul-line instead of pitching it *over* the foul-line and out on the lane.

It will help you maintain proper balance throughout your approach if you remember to push your ball straight out (never upward), guiding it gently with your non-bowling hand and letting it drop as you begin to move forward. The motion should be a smooth, easy, natural one with no conscious effort. Don't start with a sudden jerk. Keep your elbows in against your body as you start the pushaway, in a loose, relaxed manner.

The elbows of all of the game's sharpshooters are tucked in and their pushaways and starts of strides are simultaneous, unstrained functions. Repeat after them.

A demonstration of good pushaway form. The ball, partially supported and guided by the non-bowling hand, has been pushed effortlessly away from the body as the bowler begins his stride to the foul-line.

Raising the ball straight up instead of pushing it out and letting it drop on the first step tends to delay the backswing. This can make your body be ahead of the ball at the foul-line, in turn bringing about an improper sidewise, "around-the-hip" finishing swing. Carrying the ball too far and too long can also delay the swing and cause your body to be ahead of the ball at a point of release.

Bill Srock illustrates another harmful habit of many bowlers. Here he has failed to push the ball out and away from his body properly and, instead, has let it drop, kerplunk, at the very outset of his start. This causes the shoulder to drop or sag and brings the ball back and through too soon. The result: It causes one to drop the ball at or short of the foul-line, thus also affecting proper "lift" of ball out on lane.

The Approach

The ball you use . . . your "hold" on it . . . the stance you take . . . your pushaway . . . each offers a vital contribution to your bowling welfare. They are like the preparations one makes for an important trip. Here the trip is to the foul-line.

A sound approach is one that is smooth, even, well-balanced. Footwork and arm-swing are synchronized and work together in perfect unison. There is no jerking motion, strain or tension. At the end of your brief, leisurely jaunt to the foul-line your sliding foot and bowling hand will have reached the dividing line between approach and lane at precisely the same time and you will be tuned for proper release and follow-through.

Remember to hold the ball easily, but firmly, and move forward in a straight line. Don't hurry the start. Keep your body parallel with the foul-line, eyes straight ahead. Beware of zig-zagging or fading to the right or left. Groove your steps. Try for machine-like consistency. Begin and end on the same straight line. Don't run too fast or walk too slowly. Approach the foul-line in a brisk glide.

The arm-swing should be like a pendulum —straight back and straight out, with the left (non-bowling) arm extended for proper balance. Height of the backswing should be somewhere between belt and shoulder line. Let the forward momentum develop itself.

As with other phases, after a while your approach will get to feel natural, become automatic. You will quit thinking about your feet and the arm-swing and concentrate wholly on lane, direction and pins.

Throughout the approach your knees should be slightly bent, body relaxed, shoulders reasonably straight. Don't force your swing, either backward or forward. Let the weight of the ball and the law of gravity do all the work. The ball will swing back and come forward by itself. *Never* force it.

The majority of the nation's high average bowlers take four, four-and-a-half, or five steps to the foul-line. The number of steps is relatively unimportant. What counts is proper co-ordination, the fullest utilization of one's body.

The four-and-a-half step approach is broken down into the following basic components, in proper sequence:

1. The take-off is a half step or short glide starting with the left foot (sometimes little more than lifting up your foot slightly and gently setting it down again) to set you in proper motion;

2. Ball hits bottom of downward arc on first *full* step;

3. Ball starts into backswing on second full step;

4. Ball reaches top of backswing on third full step;

5. Ball comes forward on fourth and final full step at same instant that the left or sliding foot nears the foul-line.

The five-step delivery is virtually the same as the four-and-a-half step delivery. The main difference, of course, is in the first step, which is a *full* one in the five-step approach. A word of caution about the five-step delivery: Maintain an unhurried gait.

In the four-step approach, the first step is a full one taken with the *right* foot. Synchronization of arm-swing and footwork varies little in the four, four-and-a-half and five-step deliveries.

Tom Hennessey and Robbie Frey are at once famous and envied for their perfect footwork and timing. Their first step, blending with the pushaway, is easy-going and casual, not one that suggests the beginning of a race or a high-stepping march. They achieve balance and rhythm by practicing what they preach: Keep the swing pendulum-straight, arm and wrist fairly rigid, toe pointed straight ahead. At release, the body should be pitched forward. Stay down with the ball and reach out for the target, letting the armswing run its full, natural course.

The differences between these three deliveries are slight and actually of little real importance to most bowlers. Use whichever you find to be the easiest and most natural for you.

The lesser-used three-step delivery starts with a full step taken with the left foot. The ball is lowered almost immediately. It goes into the backswing on the second step and is brought down and out on the third and final slide step. This is the least recommended of all approaches. Though shorter than the more commonly used deliveries—only eight to ten feet—the strides are longer, with the forward

swing somewhat delayed. More strain and effort are involved and more miscues in timing are likely to occur in the three-step delivery.

Though we have explained it here, don't occupy yourself too much with where the ball will be at certain given points of your approach. It will only confuse and keep you from concentrating on other more important things. Start out correctly and it's better than an even bet that your footwork and arm-swing will hit it off fine together without further concern on your part.

A final word of approach advice: Don't fool with trick styles, or try to be "fancy," or mimic a delivery that might be unnatural for you. Develop your own natural, unpretentious method. Remember that a simple, direct, uncluttered delivery is the most effective delivery of all.

In the proper backswing the ball never goes higher than your shoulder or below the hips. Note the straight arm that helps one bring the ball through in the same pendulum-like, grooved-swing fashion every time. Observe also the forward press which will help the body bring the arm and ball forward effortlessly at the instant of release. There's no sloppiness here!

"It don't mean a thing if you ain't got that swing," paraphrases Billy Golembiewski. Learn to swing as consistently, smoothly and effortlessly as the pendulum on a clock, and you have mastered half of the problems of bowling. The pendulum-like arm motion should begin at start of downswing. Maintained freely and naturally, it should be kept in line with your target throughout delivery and release.

The Finishing Slide And The Release

So far it has been "ready, aim . . ." Now comes the actual firing.

The slide and the release, like everything else in bowling, should be easy and unaffected, a dovetailing of functions devoid of any undue strain.

As the ball is about to be rolled, your eyes should be fastened on the target, your arm and wrist rigidly straight, your shoulders parallel to the foul-line. (Beware of a loose wrist, cocking your wrist, crooking your elbow or dropping your shoulder.)

The left arm should be extended naturally to aid balance. Your right leg should swing around in back of you in line with, or slightly past, your left hip pocket to further enhance balance, to check momentum and to absorb some of the braking stress. The sliding toe should be pointed straight ahead, the left leg bent slightly at the knee, the body bent at the waist. Don't hurry the arm-swing, but a gradually increased acceleration of it is desirable.

The fingers of your bowling hand should be under the side of the ball, with the thumb pointing to approximately "11 o'clock." At the instant of release, care should be taken to keep your eyes glued to your target (either the pins or a spot on the lane). Don't pull back or jerk up. Keep your head and body down and forward. *Stay with the ball,* arm stretched out and directed at target, until the release and follow-through have been fully completed.

When the ball leaves your hand the thumb should—by itself, without your thinking about it—come out first. It is not necessary to turn or twist your hand in any manner whatsoever to put "stuff" on your ball. The job will be done for you, and properly, by the grip of your fingers and your swing-out motion alone. The correct finger action at this stage can be likened to squeezing a trigger, milking, or tossing a spiral. The firmly-pressed, clinging fingers, coupled with the natural momentum of the follow-through, when the arm-swing is brought out and up at the release, will automatically impart the "lift" required to make your ball work in by itself.

The slide, entered into easily, not in an abrupt, helter-skelter fashion, should be about 12 inches long (ending from three to six inches short of the foul-line), with the ball passing close to the left ankle. Never come to a sudden, screeching halt. Along with pulling back and jerking up, this also can cause you to pull your ball to the left, out of the proper directional track.

A medium-speed ball will generate the most potency, say the stars. If it is rolled too speedily—repeat, *rolled,* not thrown—it will slide or skid instead of grip the lane as it should for maximum effectiveness. If it's too slow, the turn will peter out and the ball will "quit" before it reaches the pins, causing the ball to straighten out, or fade, and be rendered otherwise powerless at impact.

It is a simple matter to grow lax about the position of your hand when the ball is about to be released. If you turn your hand, and do it too soon, your hand will be on top of the ball when you let it go. This can make the ball drop too soon. It can cause the ball to spin or slide on the lane without the gripping, driving-in action considered so essential by the better bowlers.

Also, to jump to another common fault, if your arm-swing is too fast, brought through hurriedly in a whip-like motion, this tends to pull the ball over to the left. An arm movement that is too *slow* can harm your release as much as one that is too fast. When the swing is too slow the release is apt to collapse or be jerky, prompting the ball to drop at your feet on the approach side of the foul-line.

Failing to get the ball out in front of you, where you can see what you're doing with it, can prove to be another monkey-wrench in your bowling machinery. The ball should be literally *carried* out over the foul-line with the fingers (at this late point the thumb should be just about out of the ball) and quietly deposited on the lane anywhere from five to twenty inches past the foul-line at the extreme end of your reach.

When released in this smooth way, the ball has to go where you want it to go.

Tom Hennessey, Joe Joseph and Bob Strampe (from left) all exhibit flawless arm, leg and body coordination while cutting loose with their best Sunday pitches.

Straightening up or pulling back and away from the pins just before or when loosing the ball can upset balance and ruin the smooth, gliding release that is essential to rolling a good ball. Pulling erect at release prompts a clashing where one part of you is going in one direction and another part is headed a different way. The antidote is to bend forward from the waist during the slide, and stay that way until release has been fully completed.

A sound follow-through is one where you appear to be reaching well out in the specific direction of your target.

The Follow-Through

You've heard the old saying that "A chain is only as strong as its weakest link." Well, the axiom has a place in bowling. The final link of your delivery is the follow-through and if it has a weak spot it can make all the other links of good bowling that you may have welded together fall apart in a meaningless heap— just short of the pay-off.

A proper follow-through is one where the arc of the swing runs its full course of natural impetus. At the extreme finish your hand should be stretched well out in front of you in line with the target. It should look like you are *reaching* for your target.

The body itself, not only the hand and arm, also figures in the follow-through. The top half of your body should be bent slightly forward, shoulders just over the foul-line, in further natural conformance of what has been said about reaching out.

Since the body will be, or *should* be, stooped forward at this vital stage, the finish of your follow-through should find your hand at, or slightly above, eye-level. Keep down at all times. Don't lift your head until the ball has almost reached the target.

Going completely through with the arm-swing reduces the margin of error where direction is concerned. The full follow-through motion helps guide the ball, keep it on course.

A properly executed follow-through not only aids aim and rounds out perfect balance, but, as pointed out earlier, it favorably affects the rolling motion of your ball.

The bowling stars practice what they preach when the subject is the follow-through. They all bend forward, reach way out for their targets and come straight up with their arms as they finish their pendulum-like swings.

Avoid a "chopping short" of your follow-through. Don't let it go too high above your head, either. Don't pull it to the left across your body. Don't end with it far out to the right.

Any one of these follow-through flaws can turn out to be that weak link.

The hook-curve grabs the lane determinedly as it drives into the pins. Its constant bearing-in behaviour reduces deflection of ball against pins, prompts a sweeping, mixing action.

Types Of Working Balls

Included among the "don'ts" that pop up frequently on these pages should be one that bellows, "Don't overload yourself with a lot of unnecessary guff about hooks and curves, straight balls and backups."

If you start cramming your poor head with all there is to know about all the types of balls that can be unleashed, wondering what and when and how, you'll wind up having some spirited discussions with yourself in caged-in quarters.

There are a few basic essentials connected with the four main types of balls that one should learn well and remember. Quite frankly, there is little beyond these pertinent points which the beginning bowler, and even the more experienced one, need trouble himself about.

Contrary to what some overly analytical experts would like you to believe, the hook and the curve—the way they are rolled, their behaviour on the lanes, and their action at pin impact—are so closely related, and sometimes so mysteriously wrought, that they are not always distinguishable or fully comprehended even by the headliners.

Briefly and to the point, a hook is said to "duck in" more sharply than a curve. It is rolled on a straighter, more direct angle, about a foot in from the gutter. The starting stance should be approximately in line with the 1-3 pocket. Generally, the ball is aimed at or just to the right of the 3-pin. It travels in a straight or nearly straight line until it nears the strike zone, then cuts to the left.

A curve covers more lane. It is angled out toward the 6-pin, from a starting position ap-proximately in line with the 2-pin, and brought back to the 1-3 slot in a wider, more gradual arc.

The action of both hook and curve can be likened to a midget racing car making a turn. At the turn there is a violent skidding, then, pulling out of it, the wheels go into a forward rolling motion. So it is with a bowling ball that hooks or curves. At the very outset it spins and skids like crazy, then grimly settles into a gripping, charging, cart-wheeling vehicle of destruction.

A hook and a curve are prompted by finger-hand movements that are almost identical. When you have become sharp enough bowlingwise to employ a ball that doesn't hue to a straight line, the method you use to bring the deviation to a happy aftermath is one that should be completely natural, automatic, unforced. (See chapter headed, "The Finishing Slide And The Release" for the recommended method.)

In time, but don't rush the moment, you undoubtedly will realize your ambition to roll a full-blown hook or curve. What it will actually turn out to be, ace bowlers maintain, rests largely on lane conditions and directional angles. Thus it can be a hook one day and a curve the next, even if your method of release remains the same.

Both the hook and the curve, or, to merge the two into a truer, more accurate description, the *hook-curve*, produces more strikes than either the straight ball or backup because it (the hook-curve) has more "mixing," plowing-through action. When a ball veers in resolutely from right to left, as does the hook-curve, it is less likely to be deflected by the pins than a ball that follows a straight course or one that is falling away in the beginning. While tougher to control than the straight ball, the hook-curve compensates by giving the bowler a wider pocket to shoot at. (To carry all ten pins a straight ball in most instances has to be fitted into the pocket almost perfectly, while a hook-curve needs only to come in thin, often barely touching the head pin, to sweep or kick the pins around and achieve the same satisfying end result.)

Actually, "stuff" has little connection with the size of a hook-curve. A comparative short break, which is more desirable since it is easier to control, can be just as effective.

Angle and proper speed play important roles in the hook-curve production. What may start out as a strong ball can be made weak when it is let out too far in an excessively wide, to-the-right angle. Here the turn of the ball expends itself "coming back" instead of conserving power (not to be confused with brute force) until it is needed most—at pin impact. A relatively tame ball can be made viciously effective when it is bolstered by being angled into the pocket.

"Playing" lanes can get to be still another complex matter with endless contingent factors. But, keeping it as elementary as possible, if you find your ball is not "coming up" enough, then either move to the right and point it in (the more common solution) or move a little more to the left (center) and roll the ball in a direct line straight into the pocket. If your delivery is not at fault, and you find that your ball is curving too much, continually crossing over to the left side of the head pin, then move to the left and either straighten out your line or angle it more to the right.

The top players wisely prefer not to cross over too many boards on a lane. They try to "track" their balls, breaking same not more than four to eight boards *whenever possible*. Their theory, and it pays off handsomely, is that a "line" ball is controlled easier and more consistently under varying conditions. The trick—one that is not easily accomplished— is to hold as tight a line as possible, yet maintain "stuff". That's where the star bowlers stand out. It is the secret of their success both at home and in a strange environment. A big, sweeping bender may be a thing of beauty to behold, but it isn't worth a bogus dime if you don't know where it is going half of the time.

The straight ball is rolled with the thumb on top—pointing directly at the pin or pins— with the fingers underneath. It is released without any finger or hand action. Delivery should be made from the right corner of the lane, the ball angled straight into the 1-3 pocket. Unless you are one of those rare individuals who from the very start roll a hook-curve and instinctively know what to do with it, the straight or nearly straight ball is recommended until experience and control are acquired. The hook-curve demands infinitely more practice than the straight ball.

The backup is from hunger, and usually produces same. Its behaviour is inconsistent. It is even more difficult to control than the far more productive hook-curve. As a strike-getter it's an out-and-out failure. The backup, which fades to the right, is rolled with the thumb pointing at the pins and released with a left-to-right clockwise turn. Shun it as you would poison ivy.

Some bowlers roll a hook-curve when going after strikes but switch to a straight ball or even a backup on their spare shots. Top bowlers frown at this practice. They say, "Don't mix types of balls; stick to one or the other at all times."

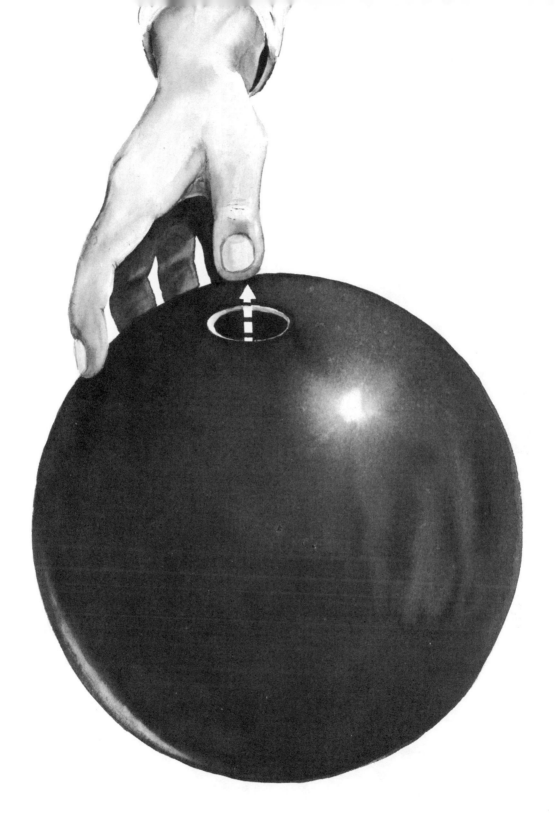

A hook-curve is achieved through counter-clockwise finger lift action as the ball is released. When done properly, it's automatic. The thumb comes out of the ball first. The ball then hangs on the fingers and the outward and upward releasing swing and follow-through impart the desired lifting turn.

HOOK BALL

The hook, highly esteemed among stars, is delivered from a starting position in line with the three-pin. It travels in a straight or near-straight path until it approaches the pin triangle, then veers sharply to the left. A hook's potential is heightened when angled in from the righthand portion of the lane. The hook is preferred by better bowlers because its pummeling power reaches its peak at pin impact.

CURVE BALL

A curve is delivered from a starting stance just to the left of the head-pin. The ball is let out toward the six-pin and its return is in a wide distended arc. Considerably more lane is covered than with a hook. The hook and the curve are both generated in about the same basic way—firmly pressed, clinging fingers and an upward and outward release and follow-through.

STRAIGHT BALL
While less likely to set the pins a-dancing than a hook or curve (or, as we prefer to describe it—a hook-curve), the easier-to-handle-and-control straight ball is recommended until experience and more skill are acquired. The straight ball is released from the right side of the lane and angled into the 1-3 pocket. The thumb is on top of the ball, pointing at target, the fingers underneath. Ball is let loose without twist, turn or lift.

'Spot' And 'Pin' Bowling

If you're looking for an argument in bowling, bring up the relative merits of spot and pin bowling. While a majority of the stars favor and use the spot method, enough of them employ the pin system to make the matter an interesting debate. It's always good for at least a few verbal rounds.

Apparently the answer is: Use whichever system "strikes" you best, the one with which you feel most at home.

The only way to find out is to try both methods, along with sundry combinations of the two—the most clearly defined of which is the "imaginary line." The latter, actually a system in its own right, is a natural blend of the spot and pin methods.

No matter which system, or blend, you finally retain after what should be fair trials, you will find that success or failure depends on several vital interwoven factors.

When employing the pin method in its pure form under normal lane conditions, assume a starting stance in which your right shoulder is in line with the path you figure your ball will follow. Keep that path in mind. Fasten your gaze on the head pin or 1-3 pocket, and hold it there steadily throughout your approach and release.

Their own private systems notwithstanding, most of the game's outstanding bowlers think pin bowling is the best method for novices.

The gist of their thoughts on the subject is that it is natural to look at the object you are trying to hit (the primary argument of all pin bowling devotees) and, further, it doesn't require a delivery that is "grooved" or letter perfect in every detail to work.

In proper spot bowling the seasoned bowler, confident that his approach and release can take care of themselves, concentrates only on the line and the spot.

Spot bowling involves more *science;* pin bowling thrives on *instinct.*

Spot bowlers insist that it is easier to hit a target that is, say, *20* feet away than one that is *60* feet away.

True spot bowlers pick a spot on the lane anywhere from two feet past the foul-line to three-quarters of the way down the lane and, after drawing an imaginary line and lining themselves up properly in keeping with it, they rivet their eyes and attention on the selected spot (usually a marker or a board that is more easily noticed than the other boards). At the release they reach out for the spot, all the while steadfastly eyeing the spot *until the ball has gone over it.* The tendency is to pull the ball slightly to the left. To make up for it, knowing spot bowlers aim just to the right of their chosen spot.

Many noted tenpin aces are strictly imaginary line adherants. This system is advantageous, claim those who use it, because it furnishes four check stations: Starting position, finishing position, spot on lane along the imaginary line and, finally, the 1-3 pocket.

Crack bowlers who use the spot system rarely, if ever, move their spot once they have selected it. They may alter their starting positions and their ball path angles, as lane conditions dictate, but, come what may, their spot invariably remains stationary.

The games' sharpshooters are impartial where "pin" and "spot" bowling are concerned. Most use a spot and imaginary line system, watching different sections of the lane, but many aim at the pins. If you spot bowl, keep your eyes on the chosen spot or lane marking until your ball has rolled over it along a set imaginary line (see above). Repeat, keep your eyes glued to the spot until the ball has passed over it; don't look up. If you find it more to your iiking to look at the pins, fasten your gaze there steadfastly throughout approach and release. Both methods demand concentration.

How To Make Spares And Splits

Spares are important; don't underestimate their value. Upper strata bowlers work as hard on their spares as they do for strikes. They have to. They know that one missed spare can nullify a "double" (two strikes in a row), and that two misses in one game require two doubles or three successive strikes to get back on a par footing. Needless to say, missed spares, often caused by being careless, bring on added pressure.

There's an old saying among the better professionals that goes, "Get your spares; the strikes will take care of themselves." Consistent spare-shooting is the difference between star and dub. The good bowler knows that if he just makes his spares he will hit around 190. One little double will put him over the 200 mark. Perhaps his strike ball isn't working as well as usual, or the lanes are "tough" and otherwise unkind to him. Spares will pull him through. At worst, he'll make a fair showing. In tournaments a couple of missed spares can spell the difference between a small prize-check and a large one.

Correct spare shooting comes down to not only aim and direction, but proper angles which govern the deflection of ball against pins.

A "cherry" (picking a pin or pins off another pin or other pins) is apt to happen with any angle, but the right angle will make it happen less often. This "percentage" is important in bowling and pays off in the long run.

Three basic angles are involved in all spare attempts. Each adheres to a time-proven rule built on the premise that you should move away from every spare (to the right or left) and use as much of the width of the lane, or as wide an angle coming into the pin or pins, as is possible.

The three basic spare angles, all designated to give you a more direct "line" and at the same time lessen chances of a "cherry," are drawn from the two corner pins (the 7-pin and the 10-pin) and the center pin (the 5-pin). The proper 7-pin angle starts from the opposite (right hand) corner of the lane. The correct 10-pin angle originates from the left side of the lane. One should cover the 5-pin from a center angle, similar to one's strike line.

The acuteness of the angle rests, of course, on the type of ball you roll. When rolling from the left side of the lane to the right, your ball usually cleaves a straight trail. It tends to veer more to the left, however, when following a right-to-left course.

When properly applied, the three basic angles, or slight variations thereof, will nicely take care of any spare leave. Just remember to play an angle where the behaviour of the ball as it hits the pins will be one where either the driving-in action or the deflection of the ball (depending on the spare itself) will be such that the odds of complete coverage will be in your favor.

When firing at spares to the right of the head pin, high average bowlers move to the left and roll their balls along a rather sharp left-to-right angle. But when covering spares that are to the left of the head pin, they remain in their natural strike position or a little more to the right and cut down the enemy sticks

When you're doing the right things, the pins loom close and large, easy to hit and topple; when you stray from the proper tenets of bowling, pins can become like splinters, seemingly a mile away. No matter the illusion, they actually present a fair target that awaits your pleasure.

Splits are apt to pop up even when one's ball lands in the 1-3 pocket, but they occur a lot more often when the ball plows through the center of the pin triangle. There is no sure way to stop these wide-toothed (and grinning, it sometimes seems) hobgoblins of the game. Best thing to do is take them philosophically—and make as many of the remaining pins as you safely can. Playing pin percentages on splits will pay off in the long run.

The center—or five-pin—angle used when covering center-of-lane spares is one in which the bowler should address pin or pins in the same manner as when trying for a strike. Allow for angle or break of the ball by aiming at the right side of the target. Try to hit all single-pin spares dead-center; otherwise, follow the ancient axiom: "Hit 'em all with the ball."

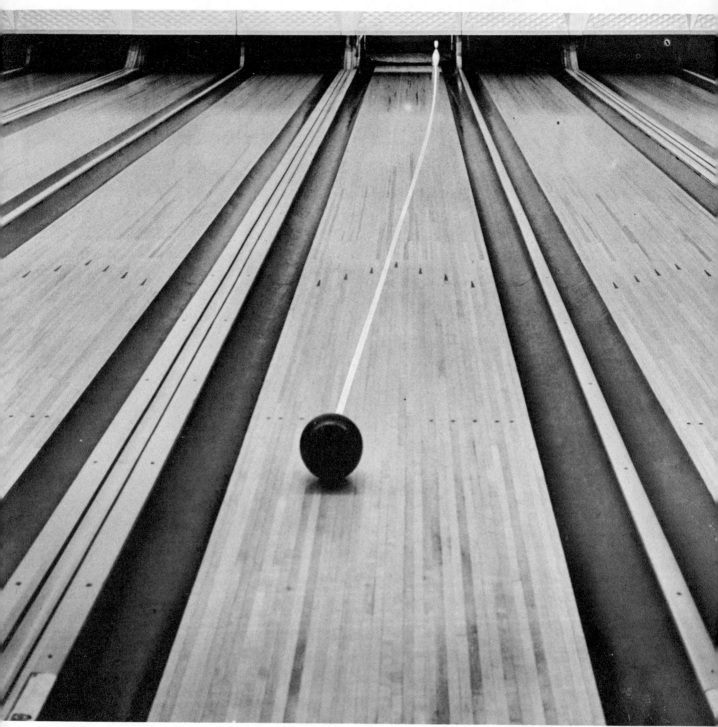

Another basic spare-shooting angle is one that follows the left-to-right line illustrated above when attempting to topple pin or pins on the right-hand side of lane. As is shown, the correct ten-pin angle originates from left side of the lane. When rolling an abrupt left-to-right angle, the ball tends to go fairly straight; don't play it too far to the right, but almost straight at the target, even allowing it to "fall back" a little. The acuteness of one's angle depends a lot on the condition of the lane (i. e., whether it takes a hook-curve readily, or doesn't).

The third basic angle for spares is the seven-pin angle used when rolling at pin or pins on the left-hand portion of lane. In this instance, stand somewhat to the right (in line between the three-pin and the six-pin), face pin or pins squarely and fire away, allowing for a little more lane coverage than on other angles. As on strikes, keep your eyes glued on the target, or a spot on the lane, and reach out with the ball.

from that vantage point. This modified angle, used only when shooting at pins to the *left* of the head pin, reduces the likelihood of chopping off pins. It further enables one to maintain a more uniform release.

Most supporters of the spot system also watch a spot on the lane when rolling at spares. The spot is in line with whatever spare they happen to be gunning for, of course, but closer to the target than on strike tosses in order to get more "lane vision."

On single-pin spares, try to hit the pin dead center. Even if you are slightly off beam, you will hit enough of the aimed-at object to topple it. Single-pin spares should never be missed.

Each pin represents a 23-inch target. A ball has a diameter of approximately nine inches, while a pin is about five inches across at its widest point. The tolerance on both sides of the pin therefore comes to nearly two feet. So don't let one-pin spares scare you!

Here's what to do to make those spares:
1. Use correct basic angle;
2. face target, shoulders square;
3. walk straight toward target (on whatever slight angle is necessary);
4. follow through directly at target, or just to right of target (depending on your angle and type of ball), whether it be at pin or pins or at a spot on the lane.

Again, percentages mean a lot in the big leagues. Under usual circumstances, the pros prefer to make one or two pins of a wide-open split of three or more pins rather than try to convert the split into a spare and perhaps miss all of the pins. Throughout the course of a season these one or two-pin collections from big splits can add up to a dozen whopper-split conversions. In short, unless a league game, the result of a match, or a sizeable difference in a prize-check hangs on the outcome, make sure you knock over as many of the pins of a split as you can.

Your chances of actually making a split are better if you *come into* the pin you desire to slide across, rather than cut it thinly going away.

PIN IS BIG TARGET

Relax when zeroing in on those one-pin spares. You've plenty of room. The pin is five inches across. A ball has a diameter of nine inches. In all, the tolerance comes to 23 inches—a big target.

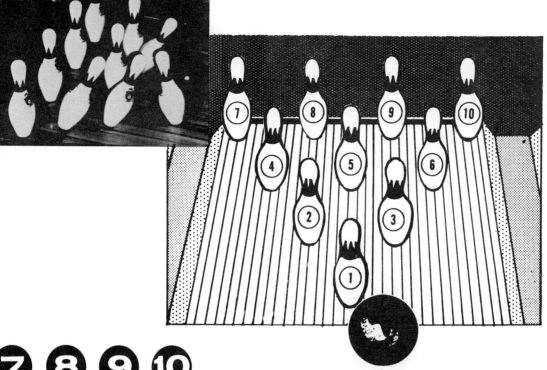

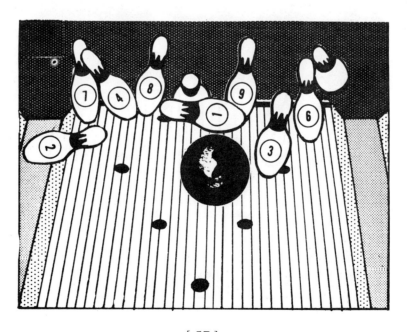

There's nothing quite like the sight and sound of a bowling ball crashing into the 1-3 pocket for a strike . . . but, until they automate even bowlers, there always will be spares to make. Making spares may be less glamorous, less thrilling and less satisfying than making strikes, but spares are vital in tenpins, too. They are the stanchions that hold up your game. You can't be a good bowler without being a good spare shooter. The following pages demonstrate recommended spare-making methods.

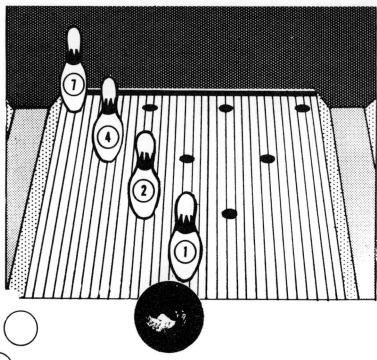

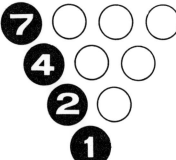

This spare is made from the right-hand corner
of the lane. Ball is sent between the one and
two pins, with the four toppling the seven.

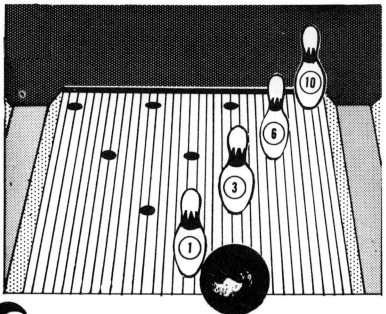

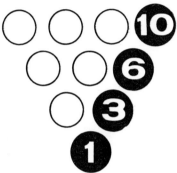

This spare is made by angling from the left side of the lane so that the ball hits between the one and three pins, the six being sent over against the ten.

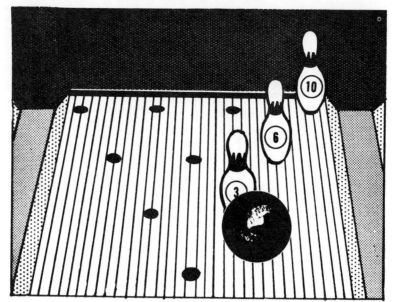

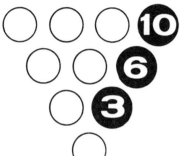

The three-six-ten spare is made by bowling from the left corner of the lane, angling the ball across to catch the right half of the three pin, then caroming off to cover the six and ten.

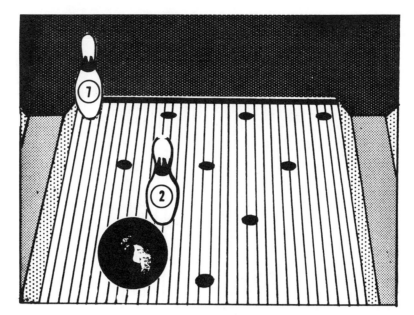

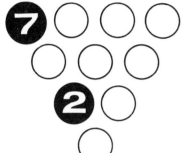

One of the "baby splits," the two-seven is less common than the three-ten. Play the ball from the right corner of the lane so that it glances off the left half of the two pin on to the seven.

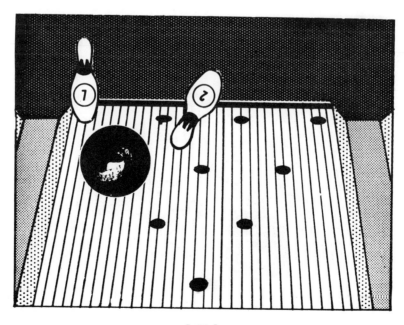

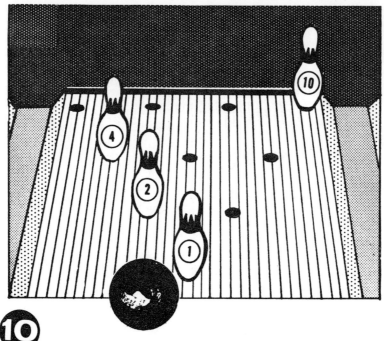

This is left when the ball, cutting in sharply, just misses reaching the head pin. Roll from the right corner, crossing over to the left of the head pin, which sails over to take care of the ten as the ball spills the others.

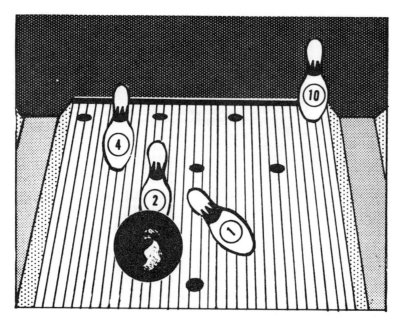

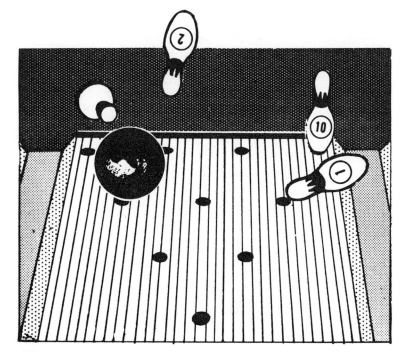

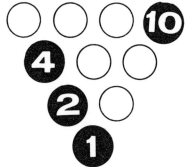

Things worked out fine in the illustrations on this page, but a little luck often comes in handy on this same 1-2-4-10 attempt. Sometimes your aim is perfect but the one pin may fly around the ten and fail to knock it over for the spare. All you can do is hit 'em where they should be hit . . . and keep your fingers crossed.

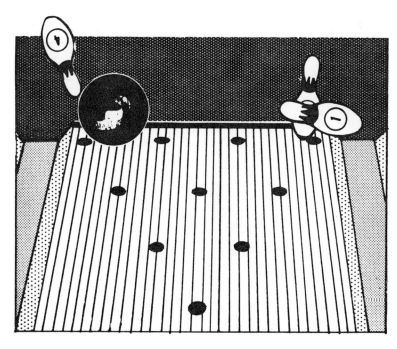

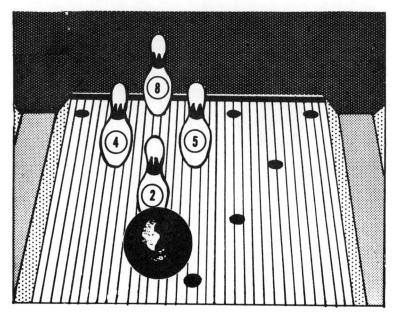

Another common leave, usually the result of the ball barely reaching the head pin. Played from the right-hand corner of the lane, the ball should come into the right half of the two pin.

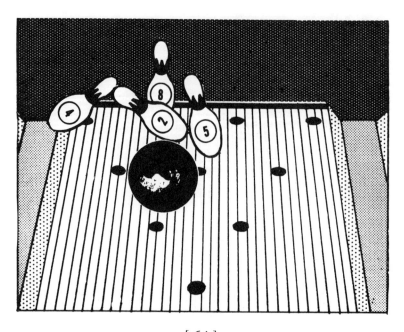

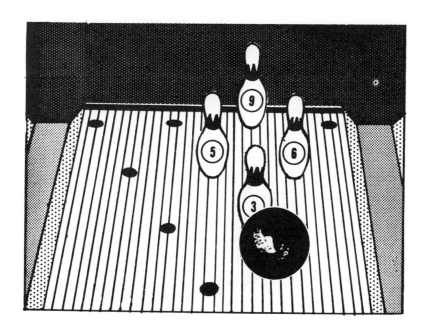

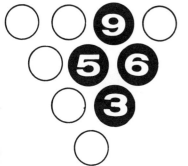

A rather difficult shot usually played from left center of lane. Try to bring the ball in full against the right half of the three. The three then takes the five and nine, and the ball carries out the six.

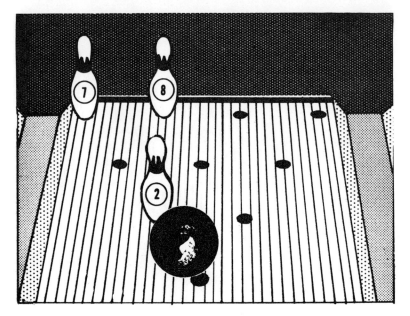

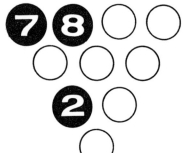

This is easily converted by rolling the ball from the right-hand corner, causing it to come in full on the right half of the two pin, which takes the seven as the ball carries on to fell the eight pin.

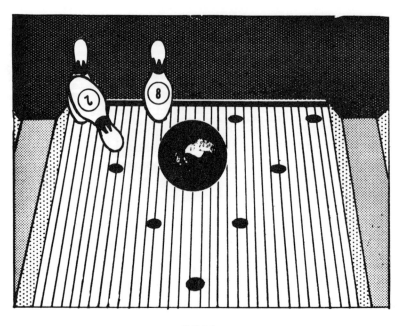

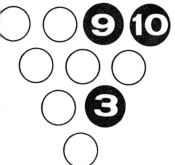

Roll at this leave from the left side of the lane, trying to hit the three pin heavily on the right side, deflecting enough to fit in between the nine and ten pins.

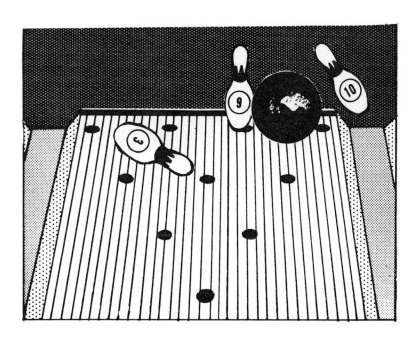

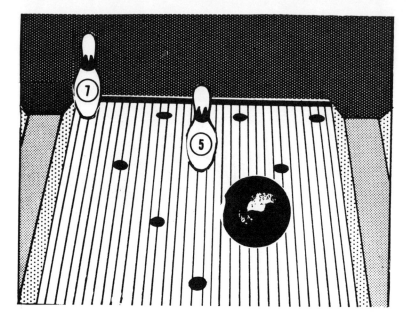

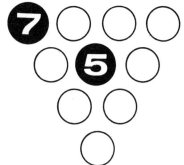

This often-left split frequently is the result of a thin pocket hit with a ball that has little or no "stuff" on it. Roll the ball from about the center of the lane, playing it to touch the five thinly on the right side, sliding it over to the seven pin.

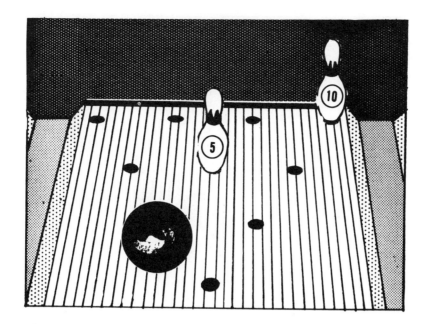

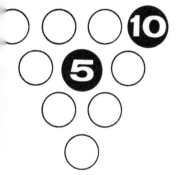

This is usually the result of a light cross-over hit, but can sometimes be left on a light pocket hit. Make it by rolling the ball from the center of the lane, hitting the five pin thin on the left side.

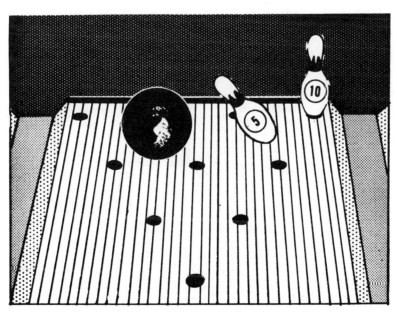

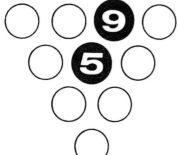

Started from about the center of the lane, the ball should hit the right side of the five pin and the left side of the nine.

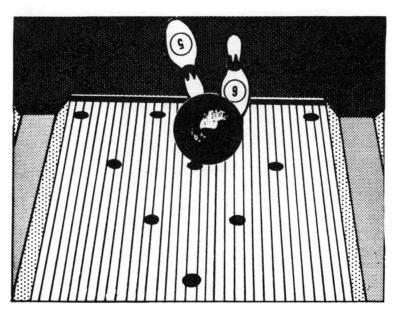

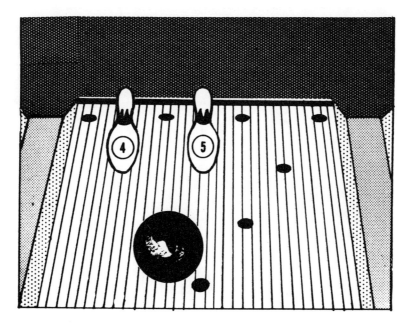

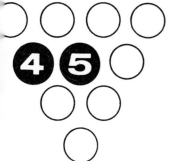

Very often a light pocket hit will cause the four and five pins to remain upright. To make this split roll from the right hand corner of the lane, fitting the ball squarely between the pins. Reverse the procedure when confronted with the five-six leave.

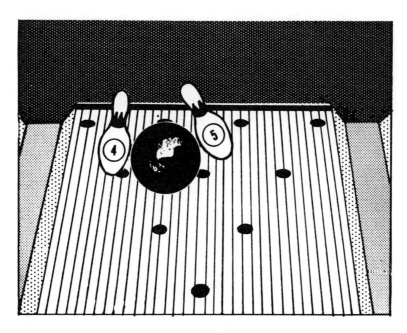

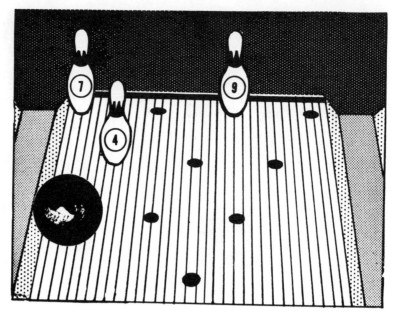

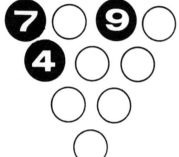

This can be made by starting the ball from the right-hand corner and hitting the four pin thin on its left side, sending it over to spear the nine.

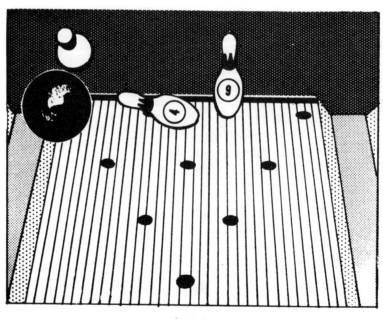

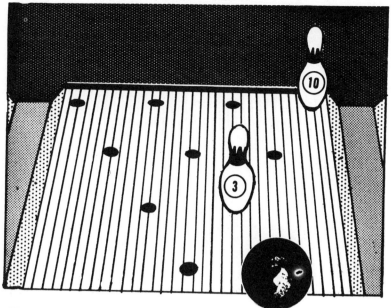

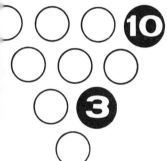

The three-ten, the other "baby split," is a familiar leave. Deliver the ball from the left-hand corner of the lane toward the right side of the three pin, deflecting just enough from this pin to nudge over the ten.

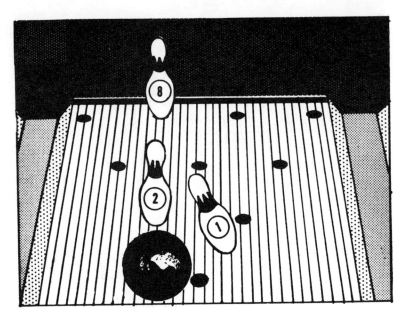

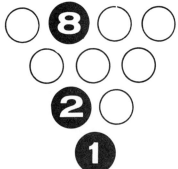

The one-two-eight, a common leave, can be made by angling the ball from the right corner so that it hits between the one and two pins, with the eight being taken out by the two.

How To Score The Game

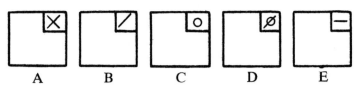

You can add to your bowling fun by learning how to score. Each game of bowling has ten frames. In each frame you bowl one (if you strike) or two balls. You can earn a bonus ball or balls in the last frame if you get strikes or a spare in it. First let's see what the various symbols mean. There are the marks you place in the small squares in the upper right of each large square.

When your first ball in any frame knocks down all the pins—that's a strike. Mark it as in *Figure A*. Each strike scores 10 points, plus the total pins made on the next *two* balls rolled.

When your first ball leaves a pin or pins standing you have another chance in that frame with a second ball. If you topple what was left with the second ball, you've made a spare. Mark it as in *Figure B*. Spares count ten plus what you get with the *next* ball rolled.

A "split" is any two or more pins (but not the head pin) which have been left standing agape or apart without any pin or pins directly between, or next to, or in front of them, after the first ball has been rolled in any particular frame. A split is marked as in *Figure C*. If a split is converted into a spare, mark it as in *Figure D*.

It's an "error" or a "miss" if you fail to topple whichever pin or pins have been left standing on your first roll that do not constitute a "split." Mark errors or misses as in *Figure E*.

A Sample Game and How It Is Scored

Now let's work out a game on paper. In frame one you roll two balls and get only 6 pins. All you do is mark 6 in the first large square and the error symbol in the smaller square.

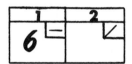

In frame two you get seven on your first ball, but you get all the rest with your second ball. That's a spare. You put the spare sign in the second box, but you don't add anything yet. Remember, you get 10 for a spare plus all the pins you get on the next ball you roll. Scoring is cumulative. You add what you get in each frame to the next one.

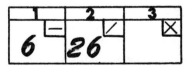

On the next ball—the first in the third frame—you get a strike. So the scoring goes like this: 10 for the spare plus 10 for the strike—that's 20; 20 plus the 6 in frame one makes 26. Now for frame three you get 10 for the strike plus what you get with your next two balls. Make your strike mark, but don't add anything yet until you've rolled your next two balls. In frame four you get another strike, you still don't put a score in the third frame box until after the next ball.

In frame four you get another strike, you still don't put a score in the third frame box until after the next ball.

In frame five you get only 6 pins with your first ball, 2 with the second. It wasn't a split, so you've made an error. Now let's do some adding. In frame three add 10 for the strike plus the total from the next two balls, (10 for the strike in the fourth and 6 for the first ball in the fifth), plus the 26 in frame two. In frame four enter 10 for the strike plus 8 for the next two balls (the error), plus the 52 from frame three. Your score up to this point is 70. You made a total of 8 with both balls in the fifth, so your score in that frame is 78.

In frames six, seven and eight you really warm up and get three strikes in a row for a "triple" or "turkey."

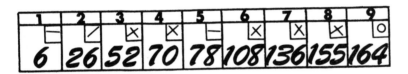

But in the ninth you get a split with your first ball and pick off all but one pin with your second ball. Here's how you add your score for these four frames: You get 10 pins for the strike in the sixth, plus 10 for the strike in the seventh, plus 10 for the strike in the eighth. That's 30 added to the 78 for a score of 108 in the sixth. For the seventh frame add 10 for the strike, plus 10 for the strike in the eighth, plus 8 that you got with the second ball following the strike. That's 136 for the seventh frame. Your eighth frame score is 10 for the strike plus the total of your next two balls—or 9; 19 plus 136 is 155 in the eighth. You got only 9 pins in the ninth for a total of 164 in that frame.

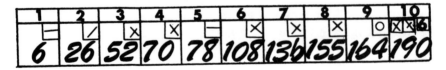

Now, let's get set for the big tenth frame. You get a strike with your bonus shot ball. This means you have two more balls to be rolled. With the first of these two bonus balls you get another strike. The second brings down 6 pins. For frame ten, enter 10 for the strike, plus 10 for the next ball, plus 6 for the last ball. Add this to 164 from frame nine. Your total score is 190. Not bad for a start!

How To Win Friends And Be Popular In Bowling

Nearly everybody can bowl, and nearly everybody *does*. Proficiency is within the reach of everyone, but not all can grasp it firmly enough to attain stardom . . . as is evidenced by the fact that a great majority of the nation's untold millions of bowlers average under 160.

However, as has been stressed repeatedly, we all *can* get the same full measure of enjoyment and physical and spiritual exhilaration from bowling. In the final analysis these are the true values, the real worth. These are the components that give the game its unending rich flavour.

There is a lot more to bowling than just the felling of skittish chunks of maple.

There are specific rules of etiquette, for example.

Violating certain good manners in bowling is an excellent way to lose friends and alienate people, besides taking some of the pleasure out of the game for fellow bowlers.

The following cardinal rules of etiquette are an integral part of proper bowling:

Don't interfere in any way with a bowler who has taken his stance on an adjoining lane. If he is addressing the pins don't do anything that might distract him. Don't start when he starts and race him to the foul-line. If he is ready to deliver his ball, give him the go-ahead and stand completely clear. Never step in front of him, go after a ball on the ball return when he's primed to go, or gesture or yell in a way that might upset his concentration.

When you have delivered your ball walk back and out of the way of other bowlers. Don't remain on the runway or at the foul-line. Use only your own approach path. Stay off other portions of the runway.

Never try to remedy sticky or slippery runways by applying what you think are counteractive substances. Never use chalk or powder. If you have to use something, get some steel wool from the manager or counterman and rub it on the slide area with your foot.

Don't let bad breaks get you down. Displays of temper only make you look childish and single you out as a poor sport. Vexed emotions can also put a serious crimp in your pin output. You may find it difficult to believe (particularly after a siege of rough luck), but bad breaks and good breaks always even up. Keep doing your best and greet all breaks with patient good nature, even if you grind your teeth down to the gums.

Yes, etiquette is fine and it should be observed at all times, but, on the other hand, *it can be overdone*. The Alphonse-Gaston role can be hammed up so much that it can tie up entire league and tournament schedules, making them run far over their allotted times. This is unfair to the leagues and tournament squads that follow and sparks irritation and resentment, neither of which have a place in bowling.

It seldom is necessary to wait for the person who is more than one lane away on each side of you. Yet some bowlers feel they must detain their deliveries until the approaches are all clear three or more lanes on each side! This "long wait" slows down the game to an exasperating dawdle, upsetting both schedules and nerves something fierce.

The lane to your immediate right and the one directly to your left should, in virtually every instance, be the furthermost boundaries of your concern. You may, if you desire to be unmistakeably safe from interference, stretch this to *two* lanes to your right and left, but, for your own sake and that of other bowlers, make that the absolute limit. When it's your turn to bowl, get up there and bowl with as little delay and fuss as possible.

Another desired quality in a bowler is punctuality. Rushing in at the last moment or being late altogether is far from being conducive to good or happy bowling—for you or your teammates. Get to the lanes in plenty of time . . . early enough, if possible, to roll a practice game or at least a few warmup balls. This limbering up, however brief, will add pins to your average.

The main function of a captain is to wheedle peak performances out of his teammates. It is his job to instill and maintain harmony and congeniality. He should encourage his bowling buddies, pep 'em up, keep them from "loafing" (a harmful habit), exhort them to keep plugging and get every pin.

A captain should never, under any circumstances, make disparaging or belittling remarks about the bowling ability of any of the members of his team. Nor should he "bawl out" or give even a slightly dirty look to anyone who happens to be bowling poorly. The person involved feels badly enough without having to endure the mouthings of a tactless captain. A wise captain "lifts up" downcast members.

The observance of certain rules of etiquette makes bowling a more pleasurable game for all. A cardinal breach is going up to the foul-line at the same time that the bowler on an adjoining lane is doing it. Wait until the approaches to your immediate right and left are clear before you make your move. And, once you have released your ball and have noted the result, get back out of the way of other bowlers. Don't stand at the foul-line singing the blues or waiting for a bolt of lightning to strike what has been left standing.

This manner of release best belongs in a comic strip. Overly high lofting of the ball can get one into as much trouble, bowlingwise, as dropping the ball at one's feet. It is important to get the ball out in front of you, but release it on the lane smoothly, lifting it out about a foot past the foul-line from a forward-leaning position in which the knees and waist are bent naturally and comfortably.

Hey, get out of the way! Both of these bowlers are at fault and asking for a collision. The one at right shouldn't be trying to steer his ball with "body English" that takes him over to another lane, and the chap at left shouldn't be bowling when an adjoining runway is occupied.

Some bowlers appreciate "advice" when they're having trouble; others have a decided aversion to it, preferring to be "let alone" at such sensitive moments. The leading teams, usually all qualified instructors, frequently give fellow members helping hands. In their case it often serves as a fast-working antidote that saves or gains pins. They are thoroughly acquainted with each other's style and each respects and values the other's opinion. Unfortunately, the same situation does not exist on all teams.

And what's true in team play, is even more valid when you're rolling a few games with friends.

Firing a barrage of advice at a bowler sometimes does more harm than good, only fanning the poor fellow's woes. If what he is doing is *clearly wrong* and you have a *positive solution,* then recite your helpful bit, diplomatically and at an opportune time. Better yet, though, wait until you've been asked. When in a quandary a wise bowler will come right out and ask to be straightened out.

Since you'll get advice whether you ask for it or not, you'd best adopt a tolerant attitude. After all, it's meant to help. Listen and weigh the value of the suggestion. If it sounds plausible, give it a whirl. You've nothing to lose; you're doing badly anyway. If it sounds like it won't work either. Thank your friend for his suggestions—and forget it. One way or another, don't let it affect your disposition.

Nobody wants a perpetual sour-puss, grumbler or moaner for a teammate. Most captains won't hesitate to trade a chronic beefer, even if he carries a high average, for a low-average bowler with a cheerful disposition, one who isn't constantly "sobbing the blues." A bowler who has a pleasant mien and who keeps his mates at once relaxed and sparked up, is worth *ten* bowlers who mope around the premises, become peeved at the slightest provocation and who dwell solely in their own selfish little bowling world. Fortunately, there aren't too many of these dour characters around in bowling.

Try to win fairly and squarely and in a sportsmanlike manner. When you lose, do it graciously and in good humour, not begrudgingly. It's easy to be an amiable, friendly winner, but it takes something to retain those qualities when you've lost. That's where they *really* separate true bowlers from crude amateurs.

Long after they've forgotten your feats, they'll remember you for your personal traits.

Bowling makes one want to soar with unbridled joy and all that, but this is ridiculous (especially when done in front of another bowler in motion).